Plants Need Water

By Heather Hammonds

Contents

Title	Text Type	Pages
Plants Need Water	Exposition	2–9
Plants and Water	Procedure	10–16

Plants Need Water

There are many reasons why it is important to make sure plants have enough water.

First, plants need water to help them make their food from sunlight.
They also need water to carry plant food inside their leaves and stems.

Second, water helps fruit and vegetable plants grow quickly.

Fruit and vegetable plants that are watered well
can produce lots of fruit and vegetables
for people to eat.

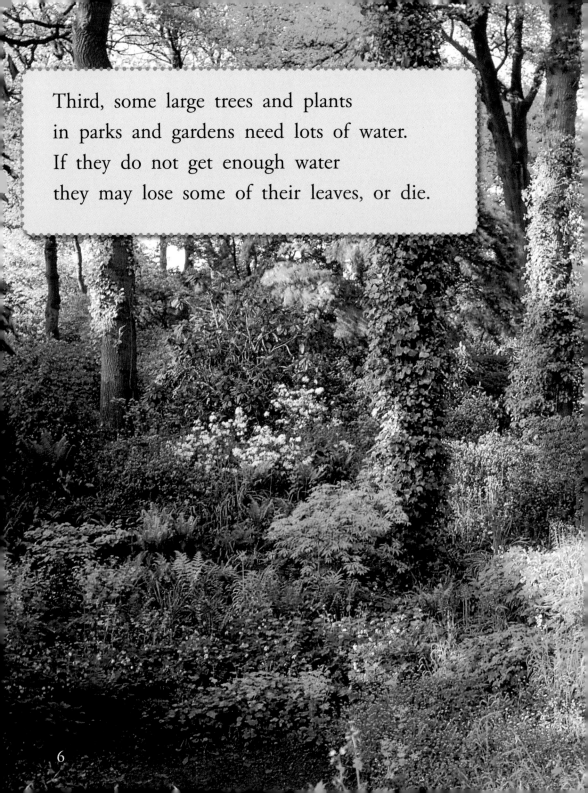

Third, some large trees and plants
in parks and gardens need lots of water.
If they do not get enough water
they may lose some of their leaves, or die.

Flowering plants need a lot of water,
so their flowers grow well.

7

Fourth, plants need lots of water in hot, sunny weather because the sun dries out the soil around their roots.

The sun dries out the leaves and stems of plants in hot weather, too.

To sum up, we must give plants water so they can continue to live and grow.

Plants and Water

Goal

To demonstrate how water travels inside plants.

Materials

You will need:

- a 15 centimetre stick of celery with leaves

- a tall glass

- water

- red food dye

- a sheet of white kitchen paper

- a knife

- an adult to help.

Steps

1. Half fill the glass with water.

2. Add several drops of the food dye to the water until it is red.

3. Put the celery stick into the glass of coloured water.

4. Check the celery stick every three hours.

13

5. After one day,
take the celery stick
out of the glass.

6. Put the celery stick
on the paper towel.

7. Ask an adult to cut the celery stick in half.

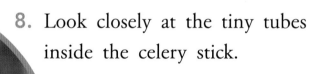

8. Look closely at the tiny tubes inside the celery stick.

Observation

- After three hours,
  the bottom part of the celery stick
  started to turn red.

- By the end of one day,
  most of the celery leaves
  were dyed red.

Conclusion

Plants suck water up into their stems.